Grandma
Says Yes

by Donna Warren

Illustrated by Katherine Collier

WestBow Press books may be ordered through booksellers or by contacting:

WestBow Press
A Division of Thomas Nelson & Zondervan
1663 Liberty Drive
Bloomington, IN 47403
www.westbowpress.com
1 (866) 928-1240

Interior Image Credit: Katherine Collier

Scriptures taken from the Holy Bible, New International Version®, NIV®. Copyright © 1973, 1978, 1984, 2011 by Biblica, Inc.™ Used by permission of Zondervan. All rights reserved worldwide. www.zondervan.com The "NIV" and "New International Version" are trademarks registered in the United States Patent and Trademark Office by Biblica, Inc.®

ISBN: 978-1-9736-9617-9 (sc)
ISBN: 978-1-9736-9616-2 (e)

Library of Congress Control Number: 2020911989

Print information available on the last page.

WestBow Press rev. date: 07/22/2020

Send your ideas for adventures with grandpa and you just might see them in Donna's next book.
Grandpa Says No-one loves you like I do.
Send to-BooksbyGrandmaDonna@gmail.com

WESTBOW
PRESS®
A DIVISION OF THOMAS NELSON
& ZONDERVAN

Dedication

This book is dedicated in remembrance of my grandmothers, Goldie and Helen. I am so thankful for all the yeses they said to me. Also to my mom, Joan, for the love she continues to share with her 14 grandchildren and 20 great grandchildren.

With love and dedication to Carter and Landon, my grandsons. May we continue to make life an adventure.

I hope to carry on the legacy of saying yes to God and sharing His love with our children and their children's children throughout the generations.

My Grandma says, Yes
we can follow this path.

Show me your ways LORD, teach me your path.
Psalm 25:4

My Grandma says, Yes
let's build a fort.

Nothing in all creation is hidden from God's sight.
Hebrews 4:13

My Grandma says, Yes
we can go to the zoo.

This is the day the Lord has made,
let us rejoice and be glad in it.
Psalm 118:24

My Grandma says, Yes
that cloud looks like a dinosaur.

"Be still and know that I am God;"

Psalm 46:10

My Grandma says, Yes
you can play with my jewelry.

My Grandma says, Yes
you are a superhero.

I am fearfully and wonderfully made;
Psalm 139:14

My Grandma says, Yes
we can have a tea party.

A friend loves at all times.
Proverbs 17:17

My Grandma says, Yes
I'll read that book again
                    and again
                        and again.

Love is patient, love is kind.
1 Corinthians 13:4

My Grandma says, Yes
God made the stars.

In the beginning God created the heavens and the earth. Genesis 1:1

My Grandma says, Yes
we can play in the rain.

I have set my rainbow in the clouds.
Genesis 9:13

My Grandma says, Yes
you can play in the bath tub.

My Grandma says, Yes those are signs of spring.

There is a time for everything, and a season for every activity under the heavens: Ecclesiastes 3:1

Jesus Loves Me

Authors: Anna Barlett Warner
William Batchelder Bradbury

Jesus loves me this I know
For the Bible tells me so
Little ones to Him belong
They are weak but He is strong

Yes, Jesus loves me
Yes, Jesus loves me
Yes, Jesus loves me

The Bible tells me so

My Grandma says, Yes
Jesus Loves Me

Let the children come to me.
Matthew 19:14

My Grandma says, Yes
I will always love you.

Place your photo here

Children's children are a crown to the aged.
Proverbs 17:6

About the author

Donna Warren has loved children her whole life but it is true, there is no love like that for a grandchild. She lives in Loveland, Colorado near her 5 children and 2 grandsons. She is hoping for more...grandchildren and books in her future.

Donna writes about adventures she has shared with her grandchildren and the opportunities God has given her to share Jesus' love with them.

Grandma Says Yes is Donna's first published children's book.

About the illustrator

Katherine Collier, Donna's daughter, received her fine arts degree from Colorado State University. Her work has touched many lives in Northern Colorado. *Grandma Says Yes* is her picture book debut. Her water color illustrations draw the readers into the story as they see themselves as the characters.

Printed in the United States
by Baker & Taylor Publisher Services